CURTIS INTERNATIONAL
PORTRAITS OF GREATNESS

•

General Editor
Enzo Orlandi

Text by
Adelaide Murgia

Translator
C. J. Richards

Published by
ARNOLDO MONDADORI EDITORE
and
THE CURTIS PUBLISHING COMPANY

300

THE LIFE & TIMES OF
CHOPIN

CP

CURTIS BOOKS
A division of
The Curtis Publishing Company
Philadelphia . New York

A LIFELONG NOSTALGIA FOR POLAND

The first piece of music Chopin composed, when he was eight years old, was a polonaise; the last piece, a mazurka. These two compositions are indicative of the love for his homeland that was so often expressed in his music, although he chose to live as an exile. He left home one day at dusk, the hour of "zal" (Polish for homesickness). And, although he was to die of it in Paris, this homesickness was the very mainspring of his inspiration. Without this, a handful of his native soil, and the cherished portraits of those he left behind, he could not have carried on. Nor would he have gone on composing. Remoteness was the essence of his inspiration. Chopin found that in order to sustain life, he needed to look upon life as a mosaic from which certain pieces were missing, irretrievably lost in time. (Nietzsche's words could well be applied to him: "The magic of music is identified with the language of our past.")

The voluntary exile was a deeply patriotic Pole whose roots remained in his native province. When Chopin left Poland he took with him some of the anguish of a land constantly being overrun by armies. Throughout the centuries Poland had been the prey of its neighbors. It is to his credit that he never capitalized on his position as an exile, on his love for his homeland; he never played the part of national prophet, although he was urged on all sides to do so. In this respect he was unlike many of his contemporaries. No role could have been more alien to his nature. The great musician, who was destined to give such eloquent expression to homesickness in the musical patterns native to his country—polonaises and mazurkas—never attempted to do more than express his own feelings, his need to remember, his reasons for having left home. He recaptured the flavor of ancient Slavic legends in his ballades and in his last polonaises, Opus 44 (1841) and Opus 53 (1843). These are songs of love for his country in mourning, songs that have never been surpassed in their poignancy; but they were composed primarily for himself, not for others. The concept of national art—the vehicle for the feelings of a nation—does not allow for the solitary voice of the artist. Chopin's life was a perpetual journey through memory, a constant seeking for the past. And he found it in his polonaises and mazurkas.

Portrait of Frédéric Chopin (left) by Miroszewski. The son of a Polish lady and of a French emigrant, Chopin was born in Poland in 1810. He left his home when he was about 20, never to return. He settled in Paris, where he lived for most of the rest of his life. Keenly aware of his dual heritage and of his uprooting, he suffered perpetual pangs of homesickness. His nostalgia for his birthplace lives on in his music. Above: The Palace of the Majority in Warsaw in a painting by Bellotto (at the National Museum).

Opposite page: Catherine II of Russia. The Empress, in collusion with Prussia and Austria, promoted the dismemberment of Polish territory in successive stages. These have come down in history as the three partitions of Poland (1772, 1793, 1795). Thaddeus Kosciuszko (bottom of page) was the leader of the heroic and ill-fated Polish revolution of 1794, which was fought "not for the nobility but for the freedom

of the whole nation." At Raclavitz, with his regulars, he held at bay the army of the Empress. A perennial fugitive and exile, he was always on the side of the oppressed. He gave the lands he had been given as a present in America to the Negroes. He died in Switzerland in 1817 when Chopin was seven years old. Opposite page: Two old prints of Wroclaw and Poznan, the latter typically Polish.

5

Nicolas Chopin (below, left), father of Frédéric Chopin, was born in a village in Lorraine which, during the reign of Louis XV of France, was governed by the King's father-in-law, the Polish King Stanislas Leszczynski (Good King Stanislas). Nicolas left his family of modest agricultural workers in 1788 to seek his fortune in Poland. A self-taught, self-made man, a good violinist, he first became a tutor to, among others, the future Maria Walewska, then professor of French at the Lyceum of Warsaw. Next to him: Justine Krzyzanowska, jokingly referred to as the lady majordomo, a poor relation in the house of Countess Skarbek. It was in the Skarbek house at Zelazowa Wola that Nicolas and Justine met and were married in 1806. Right: Frédéric Skarbek, whose tutor was Nicolas Chopin (1802-1810); he was a noted economist as well as Frédéric Chopin's godfather. Opposite page and below: the grounds and interior of the Skarbek villa in Zelazowa Wola, where Frédéric Chopin was born. Today, enlarged and turned into a museum, it is used for concerts of Chopin's music.

REJOICING
IN WARSAW

Nineteen years after the first partition of Poland—the dismemberment of her territory by Russia, Prussia and Austria—Easter of the year 1791 brought to the Polish people something more precious than this spring festival: a constitution. The nobles and the clergy had buried their differences and had come to an agreement vainly sought in the past. The sessions of the Diet in Warsaw had lasted for years. On this night the King, after having sworn to uphold the constitution, went forth in a great cortège to the cathedral to offer up a Te Deum of thanksgiving. The procession passed between the palaces that lined the Miodowa and the Krakowskie Przedmiescie, while torches threw their flickering light on the representatives of the arts and the nobles, all dressed in traditional costumes. Commoners and lords marched side by side, and the swords of Prince Joseph's hussars formed an arch of honor for Stanislas Augustus, "the King with the people, the people with the King." A crowd of more than 30,000 gathered in the square; its shouts echoed from street to street.

King Stanislas was noted for his ineptitude as a ruler. However, he made up for this, at least in part, by being a generous patron of the arts. True, he shirked governmental responsibility, but he redressed the balance by recruiting painters from far-flung capitals to immortalize the palaces, churches and wooden hovels that made up Warsaw. Even he was pleased by the agreement just reached, which seemed to bring back the Poland of better days, of a period when unity and just laws had made of it a state worthy of respect.

Amid the cheering crowd there was a certain Nicolas Chopin, a French citizen. When he was 17 years old, impelled possibly by horror of the French Revolution, he had left his native Vosges and his family of agricultural workers and carters, and had gone north. Nicolas, who had been living in Poland for several years, felt the joy of the Polish people as though it had been his own. No one, on this memorable night in Warsaw, could guess that the constitution through which Poland seemed at last to have found a united voice was, instead, to mark the beginning of years of bitterness and mourning.

A TUTOR SEEKS HIS FORTUNE

The Russian Empress was not pleased with the Polish constitution. She took a dark view of these impetuous Warsaw Jacobins, and of this Stanislas Augustus who encouraged them—a king, a former lover, and a perennial debtor to boot! The year 1795 was to mark the third and last partition of Poland. After this, the country ceased to exist as an entity, and Warsaw was swallowed up by Russia. Nicolas Chopin took part in the last revolutionary uprising of 1794 when Kosciuszko and his peasants, armed only with scythes, successfully withstood Catherine of Russia's cannon. Having decided to settle indefinitely in Poland, the former accountant was free to join the army. He was to leave it with an officer's epaulets. And, despite the Russian occupation, he gave up any thought of returning to France. He was never to see it again. He decided to become a tutor to earn his living: teachers of French were in great demand among good Poles, who expressed their resistance to Russian domination by cultivating the language of Western civilization.

In 1802 Nicolas was in Zelazowa Wola, a village six leagues from Warsaw, where he was tutor to the Skarbek boys. Count Skarbek, a wastrel and *débauché*, lived abroad. A distant cousin, Justine Krzyzanowska, helped the Countess to run her estate. Years passed, and the French tutor became practically a member of the family. A talented and enthusiastic musical amateur, he played selections with Mademoiselle Justine during the long winter evenings when the neighboring gentry gathered to gossip by the countess's fireside. Meanwhile, King Stanislas Augustus had died in Russia, unable to withstand for long the charity scornfully doled out by Catherine II. But a seed had taken root. The Polish soldiers who had enlisted in Italy under Napoleon had as a motto: "All free men are brothers." The Napoleonic storm gathered speed; unfortunately it went by without doing much good to Poland. Napoleon's last 5,000 Polish soldiers ended up in Santo Domingo, decimated by skirmishes with the natives and by malaria.

On June 2, 1806, Justine Krzyzanowska and Nicolas Chopin were married, and settled down in an annex of the Skarbek house. Their son, Frédéric, was born in Zelazowa Wola on February 22, 1810. A few months later, the family moved to Warsaw.

Left: The election of King Stanislas Augustus of Poland, detail of a painting by Bellotto (in the Warsaw National Museum). Elected in 1764, with the backing of Russia, Stanislas Poniatowski at first allowed the free practice of all faiths, for Poland had been torn by religious troubles and dissent. But his liberalism only served to stir the wrath of the Catholic nobles, who set off a disastrous civil war. The King was further hampered by his inability to resist the territorial claims of Russia, Prussia and Austria. Despite Kosciuszko's heroic defense, the Russian Empress finally obliged Stanislas to join the Confederation of Targovica and to accept the successive partitions of Poland by the three powers. The weak monarch died at St. Petersburg in 1798, a guest or prisoner of the Czars. He was a great patron of painters. Above: Church of the Sisters of St. Bridget and the Arsenal, where, in the school of engineers, Nicolas Chopin, father of Frédéric, taught French. Opposite page, bottom: Two caricatures of Polish plebeian types done by Frédéric Chopin when he was still a schoolboy. Chopin never lost the taste for caricature and for pantomime which was shared by the intellectuals of his era. Opposite page, above: Greetings dated December 6, 1816, written on St. Nicholas' Day for his father.

Fanny Mendelssohn, sister of Felix, played such an important part in Felix's life that her name cannot be omitted from any biography of the musician from Hamburg, who was a contemporary of Chopin's. In the same way, Louise, Emily and Isabelle Chopin were an integral part of the life of their famous brother, who was deeply attached to them. Louise, the eldest (opposite page, above, left), born in 1807, taught Chopin the first rudiments of French and of music. He opened his heart to her in the frequent letters he wrote her. She also published, in collaboration with her sister Isabelle (opposite page, above, right), a few "novels for the young." In the center is Emily, a talented girl who died of tuberculosis during her adolescence. The young Frédéric

founded with her a "Society for Literary Diversion" (family reading and dramatics). Opposite page, below: The Lazienski Palace. Immediate right: Joseph Elsner, composer of operas, symphonies, chamber music. He was also the founder of the Warsaw Conservatory, where Chopin took courses in musical composition. Next to him: Wojciech Zywny, a Czech, Chopin's only piano teacher. Although not at the top of his profession himself, Zywny must be credited for teaching Chopin to follow unwaveringly his own bent. Far right: Dominik Magnuszewski, romantic novelist and playwright. Above: Painting by Bellotto, the Krakowskie Przedmiescie and the Warsaw Conservatory: a carriage leaving the Miodowa, or Honey Street.

A HAPPY HOME FOR THE PRODIGY

Far left, above: The National Theater of Warsaw in a lithograph by Lemercier; next to it, the Lyceum that Chopin attended. His father, wisely, never even considered exploiting him as a musical prodigy. Last: The City Square in Warsaw. Below, left: The Wilanow Palace, a painting by Bellotto.

The house of Nicolas Chopin, former accountant, former army officer and, from 1810 on, professor of French at the Warsaw Lyceum and at the Military School, was known throughout the city. Sometimes a small open carriage would stop in front of the house. The Russian General Kuruta would explain courteously each time that he had come by order of the Grand Duke to escort to the Bruhl Palace the young piano prodigy, Frédéric Chopin. Only this small boy's music had the power to dispel the fits of depression that seized the gloomy Constantine, brother of the Czar and commander-in-chief of the new Polish army. The "little Polish Mozart" would sit at the piano and improvise, as he often did, in the drawing rooms of the Czartoryski Princes, Count Potocki, the Sapiehas, and the Radziwills. He was the talk of Warsaw. And he was proudly shown off before dignitaries visiting the capital, from the Russian Czarina, Maria Teodorovna, to the Polish composer and friend of Goethe's, Maria Szymanowska, another bright star in the Polish firmament. The *Literary Journal* of February 1818 wrote about a polonaise by Frédéric Chopin, aged eight: "Geniuses are born in our country also, but the lack of publicity hides them from the public."

Chopin in his early youth showed a talent for caricature as well as for musical composition. He also had a taste for comedy, and staged several plays with his sister Emily as co-author and co-director. It was a happy childhood never to be forgotten: summers in Szafarnia, Christmas with "oplatki" (wafers traditionally served at this time) and honey: "May God grant that in a year we can again share the breaking of these wafers . . ." The Chopin house was always filled with people and music. On Mme Chopin's Thursdays, the young people danced while she played the piano. And in the drawing room, the regulars gathered: Linde, the rector of the Lyceum; Elsner, the national composer; Soliva, holder of the chair of music at the Conservatory; Brodzinski, the poet, who lived in the apartment below; Zywny, the Czech piano teacher. They played whist, and talked: about the Atheneum recently inaugurated in Warsaw; about the new Grand Duchy of Poland, whose titular head was the irascible Czar Alexander of Russia, against whom even Napoleon's Guard had broken. Then, in April 1821, Frédéric dedicated a farewell polonaise to his teacher Zywny, who said he had nothing more to teach him. They remained great friends. From 1823 to 1826, Chopin studied at the Warsaw Lyceum. This was another happy period of his life.

Above: Alexander I of Russia. In 1815 he signed with Austria and Prussia the Treaty of the Holy Alliance and had the Grand Duchy of Warsaw assigned to him. He liked to pose as a liberal. Nonetheless his plenipotentiaries in Warsaw—his brother Constantine and the "Special Commissary" Novolsitov—made themselves exceedingly unpopular, especially after the demotion of Major Valerian Lukasinski, instigator of a resistance movement. However, when the Czar visited Warsaw in April 1825, the city, after so many years of mourning, was the scene of brilliant balls and gala performances. Naturally, the "foremost Polish pianist," the 15-year-old Chopin, was called on to give a public recital on the aeolomelodicon, a strange instrument invented by Brummer and Hofman. The Czar showed his imperial pleasure by bestowing diamond rings upon the industrious citizenry.

Princess Louise and Prince Anton Radziwill, in a print by Sintzenich. Chopin spent many pleasant summers in their castle, Antonin, where he played the piano with the feudal Prince, a great music lover (to whom he later dedicated a trio), and with his two daughters, Wanda and Elise. The latter did the profile, below, of Chopin at the piano.

A NEW STAR ON THE MUSICAL HORIZON

Having finished his studies at the Lyceum in 1826, Chopin went on to the Warsaw Conservatory to complete his musical education. He worked hard at musical composition and at the same time started his sentimental education. In 1829 he went to Vienna; for some time Nicolas Chopin had been saving up for this trip which was to mark his son's real debut in the world of music. Vienna was then the official center of artists and critics who wanted to make their mark in the world. The publisher Hans Haslinger had already set up in St. Stephen Square a large poster of the Polish pianist proclaiming "the new star of the north." Chopin didn't let this reception go to his head. He wrote home: "What reassures them is that I am not after their money and that I shall not request an honorarium." He had a tremendous success on August 11 at the Kaerntnerthor Theater. Only one lady, in the first row, gave voice to her disappointment at the pianist's look of frailty; she plainly did not know that pallor was fashionable in romantic circles. A second concert was requested. This time the orchestra did not refuse to decipher his Variations, Op. 2 and the Krakowiak Rondo, Op. 14. It was a triumph. Lichnowsky, Beethoven's great friend, led the applause. "An artist, unheralded, has appeared on the musical horizon much like a brilliant meteor," wrote the authoritative *Allgemeine Musikalische Zeitung*. Only one critic objected to the aspects of his technique, which were to remain the hallmark of Chopin's piano playing: the delicacy of his touch, the softness of his tone, the lack of dash and brilliance much favored by the public, and his indifference to the preferences of the audience. "Here they are accustomed to the loud blare of virtuosi, but this is my way of playing, and I know that artists and women like it," Chopin wrote. Already he looked upon Czerny, the plodding Czech virtuoso, with ironic kindliness: "The good man shows greater finesse than do his compositions."

The two concerts that Chopin gave in Warsaw the following year established him as Poland's most representative musician. This time he played the Concerto in F minor, Costantia's concerto; and Costantia Gladkowska, his first schoolboy love, blue-eyed and blonde, smiled at him from a box at the National Theater. For once the opera singer was not surrounded by the junior Russian officers who were always buzzing around her.

Heading the list of his youthful muses were Elise and Wanda Radziwill. He wrote about Wanda: "What a pleasure to place her little fingers on the keyboard!" But Costantia Gladkowska (right), an opera singer, was his first love. After Chopin had left the country in 1831, Costantia married the wealthy Joseph Grabowski. She soon became blind and ended her days in bitterness. She survived Chopin by 40 years.

Left: Prince Radziwill's study at Antonin—another sketch by Elise Radziwill. Prince Anton Radziwill, a prototype of the bel-esprit, a talented dilettante, a cellist and tenor, had composed some music for Goethe's Faust. He always took a great interest in Chopin. It was also said, although there is no evidence supporting this, that the Prince helped to pay for the young musician's education.

It was greatly to the credit of Stanislas Poniatowski that he had summoned to Warsaw Bernardo Bellotto, born in Venice in 1720, nephew and student of A. Canal, and known, like him, as Canaletto. Bellotto painted many views of Warsaw (above, a street scene), which are now in the National Museum of the Polish capital. He died in Warsaw in 1780. Left: The leaning tower and the house where Copernicus was born in Thorn; young Chopin visited them.

15

COSTANTIA AND TITUS

Ignazio Dobrzynski

Angelica Catalani

Casimiro Brodzinski

For Frédéric Chopin, aged 18, Costantia Gladkowska and Titus Woyciechowski were the two faces of one love. Love was the great preoccupation of the romantics. If it caused anguish—if it was attended by the pain of separation and renunciation—that only added to the flavor of the game. They all played at it: Musset, Foscolo, Heine, Witwicki, Byron. It was a century when consumption was prevalent, and one could always count on a doctor to shake his head and prescribe the waters of some spa. Love and separation fulfilled the requirements for artistic creation. A proper combination of them supplied the anguish necessary for, in this case, musical composition. And, indeed, Chopin wrote a great deal of new music in this period: Variations Op. 2, number 3, Fantaisie Op. 13, the second Concerto. Suffering is a plant that must be cultivated if it is to flower. Costantia, his first love; Titus, the young athlete whom he had singled out at the Lyceum ("you, the most delightful," "you, the one I love best of all . . ."); the meetings arranged by Jan Matuszynski, a medical student and trusted messenger; the afterthoughts and the swoonings; all these were part of a comedy that had to be played out.

In 1830 Chopin decided to leave his homeland. He approached this step with mixed feelings. "Oh, Titus, how sad it must be not to die where one has lived!" he wrote. But on the other hand: "You are mistaken if you think that somewhere in some recess of my heart I want to remain here; you must know that I shall trample over everything that does not involve me." When the time came, he realized that he had to act quickly if he was not to let himself be persuaded to remain. On October 11, 1830, at the National Theater in Warsaw, Chopin performed his Concerto in E minor. During the second part of the concert Costantia sang, "Oh how many tears I have shed for thee!" an aria of Rossini's that might have been the theme song of their love. Chopin escorted her from the stage—already echoes from the past and visions of the future were merging. Then came wild, delirious applause. "This time," Chopin was to say, "the orchestra, the audience, I myself, everyone understood." After that there remained only one thing to do: leave. On November 2, 1830, a carriage stopped briefly for a farewell to Zelazowa Wola; his friends gave him as a present a fistful of Polish soil. Then the carriage sped on to Vienna via Kalisz and Dresden.

Top of the page, starting at the left: Ignatius Dobrzynski, a contemporary of Chopin, the greatest Polish symphony composer of the time. Angelica Catalani, famous Italian singer who on a tour in Poland heard the child prodigy, Chopin, play in a concert. She gave him a gold watch. Later, in Paris, she went to see him on his deathbed. Casimir Brodzinski, a leader of Polish romanticism, a poet and a critic. Antonia Bianchi, who from 1824 to 1828 lived with Paganini and bore him a son, Achille. The singer appeared with Chopin in a concert in Warsaw. Next, Samuel Linde, rector of the Warsaw Lyceum; author of a monumental dictionary of the Polish language. He helped the tutor Nicolas Chopin to become a professor of French. He also taught Frédéric Chopin. He caught him in class once doing a caricature of him, but all he did was to write in the margin: "Well drawn."

Antonia
Bianchi

Samuel
Linde

Sofia
Zamoyska

Wojciech
Boguslawski

Countess Sofia Zamoyska (next to last), founder of the Warsaw Welfare Society, who arranged Chopin's first concert (when he was eight). The poet Niemcewicz wrote a satire on it in which the philanthropic ladies, in order to attract attention to the young prodigy, subtract so many years from his age that they end up by having him carried on the stage by his wet nurse.

The last of the portraits shows Wojciech Boguslawski, a former officer, who gave Poland her national theater. He was extremely popular as patriot, playwright and actor. Opposite page: The Belvedere and the Arsenal in Warsaw. On this page, left: Painting by Bellotto showing a country house in Wilanow. Above: A couple of citizens of Poznan, a city familiar to Chopin; and a barge in the port of Danzig.

17

Above: The castle of Ojcow, to which the young Chopin once tried to make an excursion, but lost his way in the night. Below: Pieskowa Skola, another somewhat romantic Polish scene, in a water color by Vogel. Opposite page, top: Prague, the old city, a copper engraving by Axmann. In this "city of music lovers who are prepared to criticize even a Paganini," Chopin stayed briefly in 1829 on his way back from his triumphal debut in Vienna. He gave no concerts there. August Klengel, a successor to Bach in the art of the fugue, played for him at length. "He plays well, but I should have liked him to play better," commented Chopin, never lavish with praise for his colleagues.

THE VOICE OF A DEFIANT HOMELAND

Once he had crossed the border, Chopin's tension diminished and he calmly enjoyed the great separation. He was in top form when he improvised for the Court in Dresden. Titus caught up with him in Kalisz. The two friends reached Vienna on November 23, 1830. They rented an apartment in the Kohlmarkt. On the 29th unexpected news came from Poland: There had been an uprising of the people of Warsaw, and Grand Duke Constantine with his Cossacks had abandoned the city. The people of Poland were once more in arms, and were playing a card that again seemed to be their last. Titus Woyciechowski left Vienna to enlist. Chopin tried to follow him, but lost track of him on the outskirts of the city. He never saw him again.

Then a letter came from home: His father, guessing his uncertainties, begged him to do nothing rash, but to think only of his career. Witwicki, a few months later, was to point out to him: "You left in order to acquire glory for your country." Chopin suddenly found Metternich's Vienna suffocating. Strauss's cheerful waltzes drowned out Chopin's, which were filled with nostalgia and bitterness. Haslinger refused to buy his music. "Pay, you dog, I have no intention of letting you have it because of your charms," Chopin muttered. Despite his dissatisfaction, Chopin passed almost eight months in Vienna. He worked on Scherzo No. 20, skated, had his portrait done by young Hummel. He moved about in society, becoming friendly with Malfatti, the brilliant court doctor. He reviewed his past ("Did Costantia really love me or was she playing a part?"). Finally he left, his passport stamped with a visa for London. He went at a leisurely pace through Salzburg and Munich. In Stuttgart, on September 8, 1831, he heard that Warsaw was in Russian hands. The news inspired his Etudes op. 10. The last Etude (No. 12), known as the *Revolutionary*, was written at one sitting. It was a masterpiece. The spirit of the Polish nation in chains was felt throughout the Western world. Chopin did not grab a gun and run to the last barricade, but he was for his compatriots the voice of a nation whose spirit was never conquered by the oppressor.

"She seems to exude from the stage a scent of fresh flowers which caresses her voluptuously. Her diminishing notes could not be more exquisite, her rising chromatic scales are superb," wrote Chopin about Henrietta Sontag (above) to his friend Titus Woyciechowski. And he added: "She has infinitely more grace off stage than on, although her conversation remains impersonal." The lively soprano, who gave a concert in Warsaw in 1830 for the visit of Nicholas I of Russia, was then barely 24 and at the peak of her glory. She had made her debut at six and had been a favorite of Beethoven's and of Von Weber's before becoming the toast of Europe.

Above: St. Michael's Square and the National Theater in Vienna. Paganini (far right, by Elise Radziwill) made his debut there on March 24, 1828. The tickets were expensive (10 florins), but the house was sold out and ecstatic at his playing. Even Schubert for once had a few gulden in his pocket and was able to buy a ticket. Urging his friend Bauernefeld to attend the next concert, he said, "I tell you, there will never again be such a man here!" And they went back together to hear the "divine, infernal Genoese." Right: The Cathedral of St. Stephen in Vienna.

Above: The Church of St. Peter and (below) the Karlsplatz, in Vienna. Chopin made his debut in that city on August 11, 1829. Beethoven had died in Vienna barely two years before; Haydn had sung in the choir of St. Stephen's; Mozart and Gluck had made Vienna their home and had composed many of their works there. After his success, Chopin was warmly welcomed by the Lichnowsky family, whose house was a meeting place for the intellectual elite. Prince Lichnowsky even offered Chopin, for his second concert, a piano on which Beethoven himself had played.

Below: Painting by Boilly, in the Louvre. It was from a similar stagecoach that Chopin alighted in Paris in September, 1831. "I shall certainly stay here longer than I had planned," he wrote to a friend. He soon became a frequent guest at Prince Adam Czartoryski's Mondays and at Count Plater's Thursdays (see below); Countess Plater said that "had she been young and beautiful she would have chosen the pianist Hiller as friend, Liszt as lover and dear 'little Chopin' as husband." Below, right: Kalkbrenner, the German virtuoso whose reign in Paris seemed destined to last forever. Below this: Count Kniaziewicz, a friend of Chopin's. Opposite page: Charles X being crowned king of France (1824).

IN PARIS, "LIFE IS INTOXICATING"

Adam Czartoryski

Friedrich W. Kalkbrenner

Louis Plater

Karol Kniaziewicz

Chopin's first lodging in the capital of Louis Philippe was at 27 Boulevard Poissonnière, on the fifth floor. From here he had a splendid view of the Paris of 1831. It enchanted him. Here George Sand, a woman dressed in men's clothes, noted, "What a joy to be alive! In spite of troubles, husband, boredom, debts, family, petty gossip, life is intoxicating." Paris was cosmopolitan, the political refugee club of half of Europe. Here Poles could live in a congenial atmosphere. The Franconi troupe at the Olympia Club had a tremendous and profitable success with their elaborate review about Polish events. There were acts featuring historical characters, horses, singers, dancers and acrobats. Paris was "a city," Chopin wrote to Titus, "where you can laugh, cry, have a good time, be bored, do what you want, no one looks at you, thousands of people do the same thing and each in his own way . . . a city where the Opera and musicians are the best in the world. . . ." The golden-voiced Rubini and La Malibran electrified audiences at the Opera. Rossini was the director of the Italian Theater in Paris, Cherubini of the Conservatory; Liszt, Hiller, Herz were superlative pianists. And there was Kalkbrenner, the master of traditional piano-playing. This good German invited Chopin to put himself under his tutelage; in three years, he assured him, he would make of him something exceptional. "Chopin," he said, "plays very well if inspired, mediocrely if uninspired." Chopin retorted, "*He* never happens to be inspired; I don't want to become a copy of him . . . and many people think that it is conceit that makes him thrust his lessons on me so that later he can proclaim me his pupil. . . ." Elsner, in Warsaw, agreed—and so did his new friends: Liszt, the cellist, Franchomme, young Mendelssohn. The Chopin-Kalkbrenner skirmish ended in a diplomatic draw. Chopin dedicated his Concerto in E minor to the German virtuoso, who returned the compliment, dedicating to the rising star a set of Variations (op. 20) on a Mazurka of Chopin. In February, 1832, Chopin was one of the performers of Kalkbrenner's Grand Polonaise for six pianos, along with Hiller, Sowinski, Osborne, Stamaty and Kalkbrenner: a signal honor. "It is a crazy notion," Chopin wrote of the Polonaise. The *Revue Musicale*, however, accorded it an admiring reception.

POPULARITY AND A TASTE FOR ELEGANCE

A torrid summer, aggravated by an outbreak of cholera, darkened Chopin's bright prospects in Paris. High society was deserting the city, leaving its artists forlorn. The musician had taken to signing himself "Frédéric Chopin, poor devil," and thought of seeking his fortune in America. But the paternal gods of the Faubourg St. Germain were watching over him. Walking along one of the boulevards one day, Chopin ran into an old friend, Valentin Radziwill, an uncle of Wanda and Elise, the muses of his adolescence. The die was cast. That very evening the drawing-room doors of James Rothschild's elegant town house were thrown open to the young Pole. Chopin improvised. It took only a few minutes to make Paris society realize that it could not get along without Frédéric Chopin. The first to ask him for piano lessons was his hostess. Four lessons a day paid well enough to free him from the slavery of concert tours, which not only distracted him from his creative work but also caused him great mental anguish: "You cannot know, Titus, what a torture I find the three days preceding a concert." His music now became well known through the efforts of a number of first-rate performers: Clara Wieck, Liszt, Hiller, Kalkbrenner. Chopin was not like Liszt, that golden and gregarious Magyar who never tired of performing: "I wasn't meant to give concerts, but you are, by nature, because if you can't captivate your audience you can

dominate it." Success brought out Chopin's patrician side. "His manners were so naturally aristocratic that he was instinctively treated like a prince," Liszt reported. His taste for luxury dictated that he keep a carriage, and that he wear white glacé gloves and a redingote tailored by Dautremont. All the money he earned went into the purchase of Louis XVI furniture for his new apartment in the Chaussée d'Antin (which his friends were already alluding to as Olympus), and into his charge accounts at Chardin the perfumer, Rapp the fashionable bootmaker, and Feideau the hatter. He countered Bohemian untidiness with dandyism, his fastidiousness being in particularly sharp contrast with the romantics whom he saw at the Café des Anglais and the Café de Paris. He was constantly being solicited for contributions to Polish exiles: "It would be unseemly for you to give less than 40,000 francs, but you can give more. . . ." Here was one genius who was not poverty-stricken, unlike Schubert, for example, who was not always able to scrape together a meal. Chopin's prosperity, however, did not keep his father from worrying. "I get the impression," he wrote his son, "that you are not thinking of the future, that you live from day to day . . ." And the composer's friend Orlowski observed: "Chopin is turning all the ladies' heads and making the men jealous; he has become the fashion. But he is consumed by homesickness."

Above: Boulevard Poissonnière, as painted by Dagnan. Chopin lived here, at No. 27, when he first came to Paris. Opposite page: An allegory, in the taste of the period, which celebrates the triumphs of Bellini and the singer M. Felicita Garcia, known as La Malibran (1808-1836, first portrait to the left); Chopin, too, considered her second only to Giuditta Pasta (third portrait). Between the two is Luigi Cherubini, who was then the director of the Paris Conservatory; Chopin was introduced to him by Paer, the court orchestra conductor; he also introduced him to Rossini (last portrait), director of the Italian Theater.

A BEAUTIFUL COUNTESS

Chopin's first love in Paris was Delphine Potocka, about whom Krasinski was to write, ". . . you are Beauty itself." The beautiful countess lived alone. She had an income of 100,000 francs, a rapidly changing roster of admirers—among them the Duc d'Orléans and the Duc de Montfort—and great musical talent: she sang beautifully and played the piano. One evening she asked Chopin to "interpret her" through the piano; so he stretched her shawl on the keyboard and improvised, as if to say "you have no secrets from me." It was to be a satisfying relationship. Chopin was young and sure of himself; he was a match for the famous beauty. Delphine's life had not been a happy one; five of her children had died, and she had a difficult husband from whom she was separated. Chopin admired her unconquerable spirit. He wrote her that Liszt as a composer "is a brilliant anthologist who, in variously colored bindings, collects the works of others."

The news of Costantia's marriage did not disturb him ("That does not harm platonic affections," he wrote Titus); and in 1836, when "Costantia's" concerto in F minor was published, he rededi-cated it to Delphine. Eventually, Delphine settled down with Krasinski, the poet of the *Not Divine Comedy*. But for the moment she was the Muse of the Olympus at 5, Chaussée d'Antin, where Chopin lived, and which had become the meeting place of the most prominent Poles in Paris. Among these were a number of great poets: Niemcewicz, Zaleski, Witwicki, and Mickiewicz, who tow-ered above them all. Chopin's drawing room was often fragrant with the scent of violets. Silence would fall upon the guests when Liszt played the Etudes, op. 10 (which Chopin had dedicated to him); or when Berlioz spoke of his new method of orchestration. In a contemporary cartoon he was shown conducting an orchestra of hissing snakes. And the appearance in Chopin's apartment of his old friend Dr. Jan Matuszinski created the illusion that they were all once more living in their happy world of Warsaw before the uprising. Chopin was not without detractors; there was the spiteful German critic, Rellstabb, and Field, an Irish pianist, the inventor of a new form of nocturne, who said that Chopin had a "sick-room talent."

Left: Bivouac of Russian troops on the Champs Elysées at the time of the Restoration. Opposite page: A painting by Leconte of the battle at the Porte St. Denis in July 1830. During that year, revolution spread all over Europe, from Poland to Belgium, from Italy to France. In Paris the people and the bourgeoisie, disillusioned by the reactionary Bourbon restoration after Waterloo, rose up in arms. Their leaders were Thiers, the banker Lafitte and the irrepressible Lafayette. Charles X was forced into exile and the crown was offered to Louis-Philippe d'Orléans (the son of Philippe Egalité) shown (below) leaving Versailles with his sons in a painting by Vernet.

LIFE AMONG
THE EXILES

In 1833, a pianist named Thalberg began to catch the public's attention. All Paris eagerly took sides in his rivalry with Liszt. Heine finally settled the matter by saying: "There is only one man I should place above them: Chopin." The year 1835 was a happy one for Chopin: He now had three publishers, Wessel in England, Breitkopf and Hartel in Germany, Schlesinger in France. In August he joined his parents in Karlsbad. By pure chance they were able to spend three weeks together, happily catching up on lost time. On his way back to Paris, Chopin stopped in Dresden at the invitation of Countess Teresa Wodzinska. He had been at school with her sons, and one of them, Antonin, now lived in Paris. Chopin suddenly found himself in a Polish atmosphere; once more the past was recaptured. Everyone was cordial; "Freddie's little corner" was permanently reserved.

Maria, the 16-year-old daughter of the Wodzinskis, was a favorite; she played the piano, painted, and wrote poetry. She had been nicknamed the "dark-haired daughter of Euterpe" by Louis Napoleon in Geneva, where the Wodzinskis had held open house for a year. Her idyll with Chopin lasted for a year, under the close super-

vision of the worldly countess, who was flattered to play hostess to a genius in love. Chopin, as he was taking his leave, dedicated to Maria his Farewell Waltz. She wrote to him: "How can I not deplore that your name is not Chopinski? If it were, the French would be robbed of the glory of being your compatriots!"

The following year Chopin worked hard. (The *Warsaw Courier* had to deny rumors of his death.) He received a tremendous ovation at the Salle Erard in Paris. He published a great many works, among which the first Ballade (op. 23) may have been inspired by Maria. In July he rushed off to Marienbad to see the Wodzinskis again. Invited to the court in Dresden, he astonished everyone by refusing to play for the King. He was busy summoning up the courage to ask for Maria's hand. The Countess, suffering from tooth trouble, gave her consent, and promised to speak to her husband. Meantime she begged Chopin to keep the engagement secret and to learn to look after his health. He was to take his cough medicine regularly, wear woolen socks, and go to bed early! Maria joined in the chorus: She would send him a pair of slippers embroidered by her.

The youthful Franz Liszt (far left), by Devéria. It is difficult to draw an accurate word portrait or to appraise the role of the vibrant Magyar musician in musical history. Without being an uncompromising innovator like Berlioz, or an ecstatic composer like Schubert, or an invincible spirit like Beethoven, or an individual like Chopin, or an anguished romantic like Schumann, or an innocent like Mendelssohn, Liszt lived out his romanticism impartially between art and life. An early example of a certain type of modern intellectual, he did not turn his back on any philosophic or artistic movement of the changing times in which he lived, be it the mysticism of Lamennais or the superhumanism of Nietzsche or of Wagner. He aroused the usual amount of fanaticism characteristic of any period. In this respect he was like Paganini. Next to him, the tenor Rubini, star of the Opera. Below these portraits, the Concert Hall of the Paris Conservatory. This page, below: The entrance to the Louvre, by Bouhot.

A ROMANCE
BURNS ITSELF OUT

Victoria, Queen of England, and Albert, Prince Consort. Left: A "farewell evening" at the Royal Theatre of London. Above: Waterloo Bridge and Somerset House, a view of prosperous and prudish Victorian London, where Chopin spent some time in 1837 to forget the breaking off of his engagement to Maria Wodzinska. "One can have a moderately good time in London if one doesn't stay too long. There are extraordinary things: Imposing toilets too narrow to turn around in. And the English! And the horses! And the palaces! And the pomp, and the carriages! Everything, from the soap to the razors, is extraordinary . . ." wrote Chopin to a friend. Right: Teresa and Matthew Wodzinski, who very nearly became his in-laws.

After a trip to Leipzig, where he played for Robert Schumann, Chopin, who was by then secretly engaged, found waiting for him in Paris two letters from the Wodzinskis.

What was Maria Wodzinska to him? This somewhat doll-like child, who did not know how to love him, was to have an unhappy life. She was the embodiment of an ideal of aristocratic life, the mirror of childhood. The faces of Elise, Wanda and Costantia were superimposed upon hers. She might have provided the link with Poland that Chopin needed in Paris. This model child turned out to be only a second-rate Muse. She wrote him no letters, being content to add postscripts to her family's: "We can't seem to console ourselves at your departure . . . then Mama had a tooth pulled. . . ." The mother's letters were more interesting. It was she who begged him "to keep the secret, and to stay well; everything will depend upon this."

This once-blazing love burned itself out tearfully in a correspondence edited by Maria's mother. The Countess must have been persuaded by her husband that a match between their daughter and an artist, however famous, was unsuitable. Meanwhile, Chopin still thought himself engaged: "I am thinking of the slippers," he wrote, "and I play at twilight. . . ." He kept an eye on Antonin, lent him money, sent a piano to the Wodzinskis. But gradually letters from Sluzewo, the Wodzinski estate, became less frequent. Soon they ceased altogether.

Chopin had a bad winter in 1837; he was troubled by grippe, and even more by depression. Yet, he strove to forget his troubles. His reaction to the disappointment that scarred him for years is recorded by a friend, Kozmian: "Chopin is here in London with Pleyel, famous for his pianos and his wife's vivacity. They have come to have a good time, they stay in the best hotels, and are looking for opportunities to spend as much money as possible."

Above: Contemporary print
showing a café on the
Pont-Neuf in Paris during the
Restoration. After the passing
of the Napoleonic meteor
the Bourbons reclaimed
the French throne.
This did not prevent
the gentleman in the center
of the print from wearing
the dashing Napoleonic cocked
hat. Right: Rummage sale
organized in the drawing room
of Princess Marcelline
Czartoryska in Paris in 1844.
Since the city was the
refuge of political exiles
from half of Europe,
sales like this one were
frequent. Chopin, rightly or
wrongly considered wealthy,
never failed to contribute
to events of this kind.

Opposite page: The gallery of celebrities who gathered at George Sand's house in Nohant, a caricature by Maurice Dudevant, the writer's son. Among them can be recognized the painter Delacroix, Liszt, the actor Bocage, the painter Charpentier, the politician Arago, the engraver Calamatta. Above: The Waltz, a licentious print of slightly earlier date (Paris, Bibliothèque Nationale). Chopin's waltzes did not conform to the Viennese spirit of Strauss; they indicate rather that the composer had in mind the lesson taught by von Weber, Schubert,

Mozart himself. There was an ironic preciosity in encounters between the beautiful girls and the youthful Werthers who flitted about under the candelabra in the drawing rooms of the nobility. Could one dance to Chopin's waltzes? "Yes, but only . . . countesses," wrote Schumann. Left: Hector Berlioz, who revolutionized orchestration. Next, Nicolo Paganini. Chopin heard the Genoese violinist for the first time in 1829, when Paganini was in Warsaw for the coronation of Czar Nicholas I, and was thunderstruck by his virtuosity. His Etudes show Paganini's influence.

MAJORCA—
AN IDYLL
TURNED SOUR

The Chartreuse of Valdemosa at Palma di Majorca, in a sketch by George Sand (above) and as it appears today (right). The writer and Chopin lived there during their stay in Palma in the autumn and winter of 1838–39.

"Here I am at Palma di Majorca, among palm trees, cedars, aloes, pomegranate trees, everything in its natural environment that the Jardin des Plantes has in its greenhouses. The sky is turquoise, the sea azure, the mountains emerald and the climate paradisiacal. There is sun all day long: everyone wears summer clothes. It is hot, and at night, for hours on end, guitars and singing can be heard. There are echoes of Africa everywhere. In short, an enchanted life," Chopin wrote to Jules Fontana from Majorca on November 15, 1838. To visit this shining Mediterranean isle, Chopin and George Sand incurred debts without a qualm: he to Pleyel, she to her publisher. It was George herself who planned the expedition. She had decided that the beginning of their romance deserved a special setting, outside city walls. Switzerland was ruled out as being too commonplace. Too many others had gone there: Liszt, Simon, the followers of Napoleon. To be a true romantic, one must travel. But this time something unprecedented was called for, perhaps something exotic: "The

Orient! the Orient, poets, what do you see there? Turn your eyes and your minds toward the Orient!" Victor Hugo wrote. Asia, Africa were already beckoning. Their friend Delacroix, the painter, had managed to get himself attached to a diplomatic mission in Algeria, to the benefit of his art. But trips of such length were not feasible with only publishers' advances to defray expenses; on the other hand, Majorca, jewel of the Mediterranean, exotic, almost unknown, accessible, and with an ideal climate, was just what was wanted. George Sand and Chopin left Paris separately, keeping their expedition secret except from their intimate friends, and joined forces in Perpignan. "Fresh as a rose" was George Sand's description of Chopin when they started out. They established themselves on the island with great satisfaction. The only inconveniences seemed to be the mail and the roads, which were quite hopeless. "Ard yet, dear Jules," Chopin wrote after a few days, "one couldn't find a single Englishman in the neighborhood, not even a consul." But disaster struck. Hardly had they settled in a villa when they had to move out, burning furniture behind them and whitewashing the walls as though they had been infected. The rainy season had descended on the island, a phenomenon for which they were unprepared. And although George and her children, whom she had brought with her, did not feel its effects at all, Chopin began to cough and to spit up blood. "From that moment we became an object of fear and horror," Chopin recounted. "Three doctors gathered for a consultation (odious and how different from Paris!): the first two opined I should die soon, the third considered me already dead." And so, made as unwelcome "as Mohammedans," and without a house, they found refuge in an ancient ruined convent—a place undeniably suggestive, whose exotic aura did not, however, make up for autumn rains. No carriage could reach it, which made provisioning difficult. The moods of Maria Antonia, the cook, were equally difficult. The ghost of a former bell ringer glided through the corridors, knocking at the doors

of the cells and calling the departed monks; his wild laughter echoed everywhere.

For Chopin, it was a nightmare. "You can shout yourself hoarse," he wrote, "only silence will answer." And George Sand agreed: "Never have I heard such wailing voices, such despairing howls as those the wind carries here." Nonetheless, the Pleyel piano came through customs—another exhausting procedure—and Chopin finished a ballade, a scherzo, the Preludes. Finally, money gave out: "I am leaving Majorca, making exorcisms, like a primitive," Sand was to say. "It is a diabolic country," Chopin wrote. A fitting epilogue to this soaking honeymoon was the return trip on the *El Mallorquin*, a miserable little tub. In the hold were pigs that were beaten at regular intervals to keep them from being seasick. It was no wonder that Chopin had a hemorrhage on the French warship to which George had him transferred as soon as they reached Barcelona.

*Left: The Pleyel piano at
which Chopin composed his
music in Majorca. Purchased at
the time by a local banker,
it is now again at the
Charterhouse of Valdemosa.
Opposite page: The garden of
the cloisters as it is today and
as it appears in a water color
in the museum in La Châtre.
The ink portrait of Chopin
(upper right), done by George
Sand, is at Nohant.*

40

VALLDEMOSA — MALLORCA

EVEN
MASTERPIECES
HAVE THEIR PRICE

There is something indisputably ironic in the fate that overtook this man who, on a Mediterranean island, suffered more from the weather than he ever had in his native northern climate. However, on the credit side, Chopin returned from Majorca with the Preludes finished (and already sold to Pleyel, from whom he had received an advance of 500 francs before leaving for his vacation). The Preludes were dated January, 1839. They are among the masterpieces of the romantic period. "Written, apparently, at one sitting, they have the fast-winged pace of a work of genius," Liszt wrote. Perfect in their brevity, they are pure Chopin. They reveal the whole gamut of his creative genius, his ability to convey the happiness and sorrow of life, to capture a moment of joy or grief. His Slavic soul is glimpsed in fragments of infernal melody without relief or hope. Some of the Preludes are solemn, majestic, grandiloquent; others are gently melodic or elegiac. Technically, 24 Preludes are set out according to the 24 keys in the normal scale, whereby each major key is followed by its relative minor key—C major followed by A minor, G major by E minor, etc. In terms of feeling, they are a real tour de force, made

*Adolphe Nourrit (far left).
The famous tenor committed suicide
at 37 in Naples after giving what
he considered a poor performance
of* Norma. *He was afraid he had
lost his voice. Meyerbeer,
Rossini, Halévy and Auber had
written for him. Chopin played at
his funeral service in Marseilles
(March, 1839). Jules Fontana
(next to him), a mediocre but most
devoted colleague of Chopin's,
also committed suicide, in 1869.
"Marseilles is an old but not
ancient city, and very noisy. Next
month we'll set out from here
for Nohant; there I shall kiss
you but without my moustache. I
wonder if yours has suffered the
same fate as mine?" Chopin wrote
to his friend Grzymala in March,
1839. Center: The port of Marseilles
in an old print. Below, and opposite
page: two lithographs that appeared
in* The Friend of the People *in
Warsaw (1835):"Country Wedding"
and "Country Concert." Scenes of
this sort were a commonplace sight
to Chopin during his adolescence
when he was vacationing in the
Polish countryside. He never
forgot them, and tried to bring
them to life again in his mazurkas.*

possible by his self-knowledge. They are a series of emotional snapshots: passion, despair, hope, illusion. In Schumann's words, "He is here recognizable even in the pauses and the silences."

Even masterpieces have their price. It is interesting to compare the evaluation made by the artist and the one made by the "merchants" when these masterpieces came on the market. Jules Fontana, the factotum friend in Paris who was forever tangling with Chopin's publishers, received from the composer, still in Marseilles, a letter dated March 12, 1839: "So Pleyel thinks my manuscripts too expensive! If I have to sell them cheap, I prefer to sell them to Schlesinger, who adores me, I suppose, because he manages to rob me! Don't send any manuscripts until you have the cash in hand! Lord, what a fate to be forever obliged to deal with that riffraff. . . . And Probst, who wants to pay me 300 francs for a mazurka, is a highway robber; for the last ones I had no trouble getting 800 francs. I prefer to give them away for nothing, as I did once, rather than to have to deal with those idiots. If you are planning to become a shoemaker, don't supply shoes to either Pleyel or Probst: let them go barefoot! . . ."

43

THE PERFECTIONIST

"You are not tubercular; all you have is a chronic inflammation of the larynx; I see no reason to be frightened," assured Dr. Papet, the first guest at Nohant after the ill-fated idyll. Chopin asked nothing better than to believe this diagnosis. After Majorca, George's château meant recovery for Chopin. Surrounded by friends, he began to get better. He prepared a pantomime for the little theater at Nohant. He gave lessons to George's daughter Solange, to whom he was devoted. He avoided billiards, which appealed to the other guests: Grzymala; Emanuel Arago, a politician; Marie Dorval, the Comédie Française actress whose assiduousness in the past had caused George Sand to be known as a modern-day Sappho. And he worked. He corrected the Paris edition of Bach: "I don't pretend to know Bach better than others do, but I am convinced that I understand him." He finished the Sonata in B Minor, Op. 35; the third Scherzo, Op. 39; the Impromptu in F sharp major. After a day of work, it was to George that Chopin turned: "He consults me as Molière used to consult his servant girl," said George with wry humor. She was an excellent listener. An efficient and tireless worker who could write in the morning a manuscript she had planned during the night, she was witness to Chopin's creative torment—"a perfectionist." He shut himself in his room for days on end, wept, rewrote the same measure a hundred times. Then he would start again, yet often the final composition was identical with the first draft. George finally lost her patience. Chopin was no longer a great passion; he was rather like a third child, to be looked after and protected. Chopin, having partially recovered his health, tried diverting himself with a neighborhood beauty. At last, taking stock of their future, the couple decided to go to Paris, taking separate apartments to allow each of them reasonable freedom of action. The immediate result was a great deal of work for the ever-obliging Fontana: "Find two apartments next to each other," Chopin wrote to him. "Please also see to the wallpaper, which is to be dove-gray with a dark-green border." There was also a red sofa to be attended to and some gray curtains with a frill in the latest fashion by Dautremont.

*Opposite page: Chopin, in
a portrait by Scheffer.
Below: Two caricatures by
Maurice, George Sand's son:
Sand going off into ecstasy
as she listens to the prodigious
Liszt; and Sand with Balzac
(author of* The Human Comedy),
*moustached, swathed in his robe,
watching a performance of
the puppet theater at Nohant.*

*Left: Aurore Dupin, in a portrait
by Charpentier. Her first story,
written in collaboration with her
friend Jules Sandeau for the* Revue
de Paris, *was signed Jules Sand.
Later, she wrote the novel* Indiana
*alone at Nohant. It was the editor
Latouche who fixed her pseudonym:
"Today it is S. George; let the lady
add the last name Sand to George,
and we'll know where we stand!"*

THE NEW WAVE

In October, 1839, Chopin and George Sand were once more settled in Paris, the musician at 5 Rue Tronchet, the writer at 16 Rue Pigalle. From Nohant Chopin had sent the following instructions to Fontana: "Arrange things, dearest friend, so that sad thoughts will be kept at bay and so that coughing will not suffocate me. Wish me better health; I should be grateful if you could make yourself younger, and if you could arrange things so that we might never have been born. . . ."

On October 29, Chopin played at Saint-Cloud for Louis Philippe. Ignaz Moscheles, the German virtuoso who performed that same evening and who once had described the études as "unplayable break-finger exercises," tonight shared the King's opinion: "Chopin is unique in the world of pianists." And he received, as a mark of esteem from the Polish composer, three short études for his *Method*. Despite this success, Chopin was not content. In order to re-create the illusion of family life, he took a studio in the Rue Pigalle, agreeing at first to share it with Maurice, George Sand's son, who was then studying painting

with Delacroix. Chopin spent more and more time next door, at No. 16. Here, George Sand, who was always in touch with new political and social trends, gathered a group of people committed to the "new wave": Louis Blanc, historian and social democrat; the Republican Cavaignac; Pierre Leroux, the standard-bearer of a new kind of social Christianity and of a "truth constantly marching forward which goes from nation to nation; at the moment it is embodied in Poland, whence it will spread throughout the world." Sand was among those who, according to Balzac, were "steeped in Poland." At this time she published an essay on Byron, Goethe and Mickiewicz. Chopin found in Delacroix his patron saint. The great painter considered Chopin second only to Mozart, who was the musical idol of both of them. Chopin, on the other hand, preferred Ingres to Delacroix. Each of them, an innovator in his own art, preferred the classics. They had in common consumption, asceticism and that "moderate kindness" which—according to Baudelaire, a friend of the painter—"is always inseparable from genius."

Honoré de Balzac (below, left), a writer who rather irritated Chopin. Balzac wrote of George Sand in 1838: "I found my colleague, Sand, wrapped in a dressing gown, smoking an after-dinner cigar. She wore pretty yellow slippers, charming stockings, red pantaloons." Next, Alfred de Musset, "Miss Byron," as Sainte-Beuve nicknamed him because of his delicate charm. The poet wrote to George Sand in July 1833: "I must confess, Madame, to something foolish and absurd: I love you, Madame, I love you as though I were a child!" His "affectionate friendship" with the authoress later created quite a stir. The last is Adam Mickiewicz (1798–1855), one of the greatest romantic poets, the messiah of the rebirth of nations through freedom. Another Polish poet, Krasinski, wrote of him: "He is the twinkling light of national poetry, his works are as immense as the ages, as the Pyramids in the desert, the granite nucleus of our literature." Mickiewicz never forgave Chopin for not having given Poland a great national work. Opposite page: George Sand's passion for politics gave scope to cartoonists. The authoress is shown with Ledru-Rollin. Above: Paris in the mid-1840's: the Place de la Concorde.

A TRIUMPH
AT 6,000 FRANCS

For Chopin, the year 1840 marked the beginning of an intense period of creativity. For Sand, it marked a theatrical fiasco, *Cosima.* Her heroine bore the name of the daughter of Liszt and Marie d'Agoult, the Cosima who later became Richard Wagner's wife. Mme d'Agoult thoroughly enjoyed her famous colleague's fiasco. She now hated the couple whose fame had overshadowed her own romance with Liszt, and she had dubbed Chopin "an ostrich powdered with sugar."

Chopin had a reciprocal grudge against Liszt. The Hungarian had used the fastidious Chopin's apartment for an assignation with Mme Pleyel and had not bothered to clear away the traces afterward. But the gentlemen forgave more readily than the ladies. Indeed, when in April 1841 the gilded youth, the blue-stockings, the financial world, the aristocracy and the greatest intellects of Paris crowded the Salle Pleyel to hear Chopin play, Liszt wrote a glowing review for the *Gazette Musicale.* The critics agreed unanimously. The triumph was worth 6,000 francs: "Try reading your poetry to an audience for 40 minutes and you will see if you will be paid an equal amount," was the comment of the poet Witwicki, who, 10 years earlier, had urged Chopin to stay out of the Polish revolution of 1831, serving his country by his art instead.

Mickiewicz, on the other hand, was increasingly hostile to Chopin. The poet and the composer were destined to pass each other like enemy ships in the night, in the sea of Parisian society. They seldom met. In 1840, Mickiewicz obtained the chair of Slavic Literature at the College de France. And, having made Slavicism the topic of the day, he officiated as national prophet. Michelet, Sainte-Beuve, Montalembert and Lamartine attended his lectures, as did George Sand, who often took her place beside him amid great applause. Mickiewicz preached agreement between nations; he was indifferent to crowned heads. He also wrote for the newspapers. Sand summed him up as a combination of Joan of Arc and Socrates. Mickiewicz described Chopin as "Sand's black spirit." He disapproved of him for "throwing himself away in a glittering social life." Nonetheless one of Chopin's ballades was inspired by a poem of Mickiewicz, *Switez.*

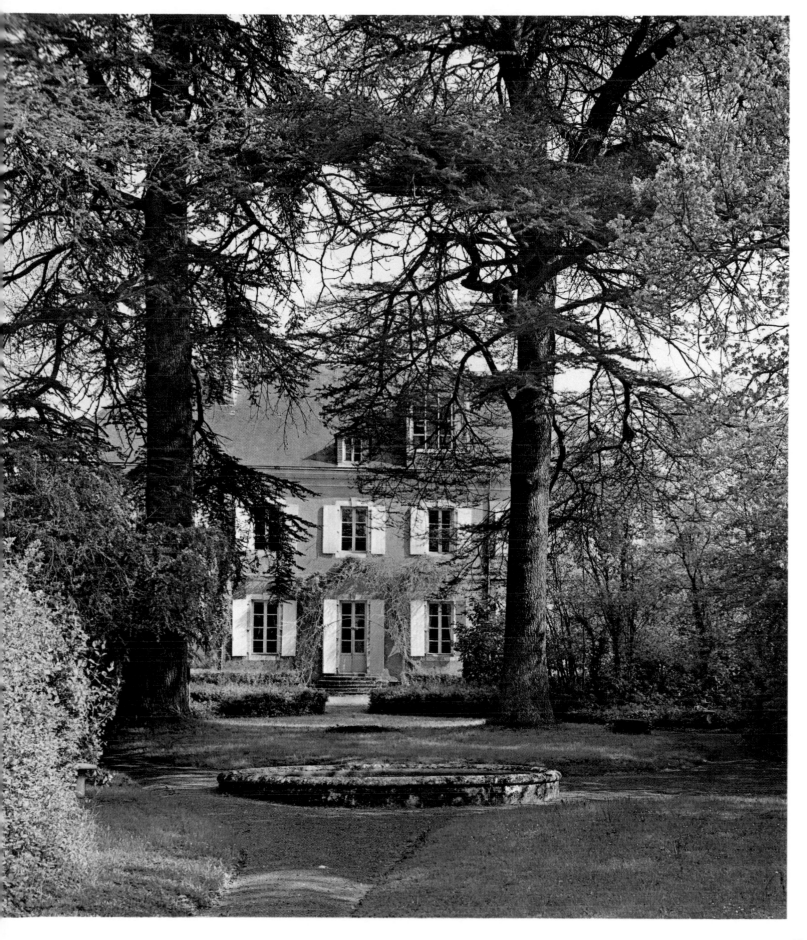

"THE ILLUSION OF THE GOOD PROVINCIAL NEIGHBOR"

Nohant in 1841: Chopin was working on the Tarantelle ("I hope it will be a long time before I write anything worse"); the third Ballade, Op. 47, in which the voices of ancient Slavic legends are mingled with other echoes; the Polonaise, Op. 44; and the Fantaisie in F minor, masterpieces inspired by his native land. He discovered in himself a certain talent for snubbing busybodies, even when they were friends of George's: "la Rosières, that unbearable creature who somehow managed to find her way into my garden, and nibbles and looks for truffles among the roses. . . ." The unfortunate woman no doubt deserved this, for she had taken it upon herself to send a portrait of Chopin—as a wedding present—to Maria Wodzinska, who was marrying Count Skarbek of Zelazowa Wola. But he struck up a friendship with the season's guest of honor, the fascinating Pauline Viardot Garcia, who was almost as well known as her sister, La Malibran. Pauline was later to marry the novelist Turgenev, her second husband. It is to her we owe the transcriptions for voice of some of Chopin's mazurkas.

During the following winter, Chopin had another triumph at the Salle Pleyel. (Mme Viardot Garcia appeared on the same program.) On the same freezing February night, his old teacher Zywny died in Warsaw. Then, in April, Jan Matuszynski, the faithful friend who shared Chopin's apartment and his consumption, also died. Chopin felt the blow with alarming force. Once more it was George Sand who saved him, rushing him to Nohant, where he was surrounded by friends. Among them was Delacroix, also ill. At Nohant, in 1842, Chopin wrote the 4th Ballade, Op. 52; the Scherzo, Op. 54; the Polonaise in A-flat major, his greatest polonaise. The creative effort exhausted him to such a point that Sand had to keep her eye on him constantly. In the autumn they moved to two apartments at Numbers 5 and 9, Square d'Orléans, the "little Athens" of the city. Kalkbrenner, Dumas Senior and a few other friends also lived there. "Let us recreate, in this sad Paris," said Sand, "the illusion of the good provincial neighbor."

Above: Fan painted by Charpentier (who specialized in battle scenes), showing a gallery of the habitués of Nohant: from the left, the painter Calamatta (snake); Maurice Sand (four-legged sylph); Emmanuel Arago (a politician, shown here as Triton); Albert Grzymala, a friend; the actor Bocage (as a faun); Liszt on his knees before Sand, who has in her hand a bird with Chopin's profile. Then: Delacroix as a shepherd; Félicien Malefille, trusted tutor at Nohant; Solange, George Sand's daughter, with a lion's head; the lawyer de Bourges, a skilled divorce specialist. And last, Charpentier. Lower left: Delacroix, self-portrait; he was a great admirer of Chopin's, a frequent guest at Nohant. "You are a famous dauber," Sand wrote to him in 1838, after having admired his "splendid, harrowing" Medea, "and, to persuade you to accept my invitation, I shall tell you that Chopin plays for our circle of friends with his elbows practically on the keyboard and that he is, in those moments, truly sublime." Next, Maciej Kamienski, Polish opera singer. This page: Caricatures of George Sand, Chopin and Delacroix, by George.

DOMESTIC
PLEASURES
AND QUARRELS

The year 1844 marked the high point for Chopin of life at Nohant. He held the center of the stage. In the spring, his father died. In order to dispel the depression of her "sad angel," George invited Louise and Calasanzio Jedrzejewicz to Nohant. And so, after 14 years of separation, Chopin was reunited with his sister and brother-in-law. The reunion worked better than any medicine. Chopin began to work again, doing a rough draft of a third sonata, Op. 58. He noted with pride that his sister, an aspiring writer, exchanged views with George on the latter's new novel, *La Mare au Diable*.

Sand herself read it to her guests. It seemed to Chopin he couldn't ask for more. For one summer he had the pleasure of seeing "his two families" together. Never had his relations with George seemed so relaxed. Life was almost too peaceful: trouble must be brewing. The storm, as in any ordinary family, broke over the children, Solange and Maurice. Solange, beautiful, restless (and malicious, added her mother),

had no complaints about Chopin. Maurice, on the other hand, did not conceal his dislike and jealousy of his mother's friend, whose interference was "unwelcome and abusive." George found herself taking sides with her son. Tension grew daily. The first casualty was Jan, Chopin's new Polish servant, the victim of the pranks of Maurice and his cousin Augustine Brault. Chopin had never liked Augustine because he was afraid she would displace Solange in her mother's affections. The squabbles overflowed from the kitchen into the drawing room. Chopin took the complaints about Jan personally. He finally dismissed the valet. But dissension had reared its ugly head; charges and countercharges flew in the Square d'Orléans. Chopin sought support from his favorite, Solange, who like him was forever quarreling with the arrogant Maurice. Sand took a dim view of the friendship between "her invalid" and her 16-year-old daughter, who "when she is riding is as beautiful as the sun."

*Opposite page, upper left:
Maurice and Solange, George
Sand's children (born in 1823 and
1829) from her marriage to Baron
Casimir Dudevant. "A weak lover,
a mere shadow at Nohant, where
George Sand's children accepted
no guidance from him," the poet
Benn wrote, in 1848, about Chopin
in the second stanza of his
biography in verse. Actually,
the last verse refers to
Maurice, who never could
stand Chopin. Solange, on
the other hand (below, in
a caricature by Musset),
was his favorite, and returned
his affection. She disappointed
him by marrying the
sculptor Clésinger. It was
even said that Chopin had
asked for her hand.*

*Opposite page: The farm at
Nohant in Berry, as it looks today.
This farm provided many of the
necessities for George Sand's
household, which was always
full of guests. An incurable
"countrywoman," she took refuge
there whenever she could. She had
inherited it from her paternal
grandmother, at Christmas in 1821;
she was then 17. Above: The
grounds of Nohant, as seen from
the windows of the room occupied
by Chopin. Upper left: Portrait of
George Sand in 1838 by Delacroix.
Below this, Liszt, Mme d'Agoult
and a friend immersed in a
philosophical discussion. The
caricature, done by Sand, may
have been done in 1837,
when they were guests at Nohant.*

"THE VICTIM" OF A LITERARY PORTRAIT

George Sand (above), dressed as a student. She had received a first-rate education at Nohant from her tutors: she had learned Latin and Greek, and had the use of a well-stocked library (Homer, Tasso and Racine were her favorite authors). She had learned to play the harpsichord and had even taken a course in anatomy. Her paternal grandmother, in whose charge she was, had hurriedly withdrawn her, after a brief stay, from the fashionable English Convent, since the girl, after a religious crisis, was threatening to take the veil. George Sand took to wearing trousers in order to save on clothes during her first years in Paris when she lived, happy and poor, with Jules Sandeau. Right, drawing of George Sand by Alfred de Musset.

On June 25, 1846, the *Courrier Français* carried the first installment of a new novel by George Sand that was destined to have a quick financial success, *Lucrezia Floriani*. George Sand always took her characters from real life: *Elle et Lui* was based on her romance with Musset, and in *Consuelo*, the heroine was modeled after Mme Viardot Garcia, the famous singer. This time everyone in Paris was convinced that the two protagonists of the new novel, Karol (the slender, sickly prince who "does not see the ground, only the sky"), and the heroine, Lucrezia ("a widow with many lovers," six years older than her friend), could not be anyone except Chopin and the writer herself. Everyone sympathized with Chopin, "the victim."

It would be unfair to say that Karol, that difficult aesthete, is a negative character. But, undeniably, a fairly explicit spirit of accusation is present throughout the novel. From the standpoint of modern psychology, the novel might be viewed as a more or less conscious attempt to get rid of Chopin. George's major complaint seems to have been that, after eight years of life in common, Chopin still seemed to hold her at arm's length. Having permitted her to share his daily routine—meals, medicines—he had always denied her access to his inner life, drawing a veil over his own concept of life and, what was even more serious, his art. Sand, an intellectual, could not help being particularly resentful of this affront. What explanation could there be for this inaccessibility? Did Chopin ever really love her? This was obviously the question George-Lucrezia was asking herself. Did he not want her to know the answer? Had she let herself be taken in at the beginning? And was this incomplete partnership enough for a woman like Sand? In the novel, this lack of communication on the part of Karol kills Lucrezia. In life also, the more vulnerable of the two was to give way: only the roles were reversed.

Above: The little theater of Nohant, where the guests sometimes doubled as audience and actors. Maurice Sand, who was studying painting with Delacroix, designed the sets; Chopin was one of the most reliable members of the troupe. The actor Piasecki, seeing Chopin act when the latter was still a schoolboy at the Lyceum, tried to persuade him to give up music for the stage. And Hervé, an actor in the French troupe in Warsaw, sang his praises when the young musician took a part in his repertory—his imitation of a tailor at work was particularly good. Left: Discussion at Nohant about the running of the theater.

FAREWELL TO NOHANT

In the *Story of My Life*, George Sand states that Chopin knew the contents of *Lucrezia Floriani* before its publication. In fact, he was in the habit of looking over her manuscripts. And it would seem that Solange also told him: "See, Mama has put you, too, in her new novel." George Sand, in order to counteract the unpopularity that all this brought her, hastily denied the Karol-Chopin identification. She even maintained that if he ever did make parallels, it was only as a result of gossip. This was an artless bit of cunning, which was certainly not typical of her. Chopin must certainly have understood at once the implications in *Lucrezia Floriani*. But he said nothing. His reaction was in keeping with Lucrezia-George's assertion: "Of all the reprisals, was not the most cruel one that he never gave up his frigid politeness?" This attitude must have increased George's irritation. Chopin was to speak only in passing of the novel, the following year, when he wrote to his sister Louise: "A work that has been less well received than her preceding ones. . . ."

If Lucrezia's complaint was incommunicability, George's was more specific: "Chopin's friendship has never been a refuge for me; all my strength came from my son." This Chopin could believe. Maurice was now master at Nohant. Work was exhausting for Chopin during the summer of 1846. He worked only intermittently on the Barcarolle, op. 60.

He reacted to the hostile atmosphere by isolating himself. "I am so tired and so cheerless that I affect the young, and when I am present they enjoy themselves less." It is quite likely that Chopin, ill, nervous, and increasingly touchy, made his presence a burden. The climax came, as in any good middle-class family, at the dinner table. As Maurice helped himself to the choicest morsel of chicken, Chopin burst out: "I won't put up with condescension." Maurice decided that there was not room for both of them at Nohant. The incident was somehow pushed into the background, but when it came time to return to Paris, George did not accompany Chopin: she would spend the winter at Nohant. Chopin left, alone. This was November 10, 1846. He was never to return. From the cold city of Paris, he continued to write George cold, polite letters, precisely like those Prince Karol might have written.

"*I have just come back from the Italian Theater: I saw Jenny Lind (lower left) and the Queen. Both made a great impression. So did old Wellington. He was sitting under the royal box like a 'monarchic' old dog in his kennel. Then I met Jenny Lind who had saved a place for me: this Swedish lady does not glow with ordinary light, there is something of the aurora borealis about her,*" Chopin wrote from London on May 11, 1848, to his friend Grzymala. Next, the actor Bocage, a celebrity in Paris, and Marie Dorval (dressed as Marion Delorme), the actress who set hearts beating from the Boulevard du Crime to the Comédie Française. Upper left: Alexandre Dumas Senior (caricature by Musset). The Dumases, who in 1851 happened to acquire part of the Sand-Chopin correspondence, gave the letters back to the writer, who destroyed them. Next is Marie d'Agoult, Liszt's inspiration. Below: The rue de Castiglione in Paris, in a painting by Canella.

Above: The Boulevard des Capucines in a painting by Stanley at the Musée Carnavalet. Right: A barouche filled with costumed revelers in Paris. Opposite page, above: Louis Blanc, lithograph by Gattier, and Sainte-Beuve, drawn by Heim. Louis Blanc (1811-1882), a socialist, member of the revolutionary government of 1848, was a friend of George Sand. Sainte-Beuve (1804-1869), author of the Causeries du Lundi, "was the father of modern criticism in France," Taine wrote. "His theory was that in order to evaluate the work of a writer, one must first know his life, the atmosphere in which he was formed, his friends, even the state of his health. He laid the foundation of what has been called the natural history of the mind, which likens the blossoming of genius to that of a plant. In this way, criticism is committed to the discovery of more than a moral truth or a literary ideal—to a historical scientific truth. There are bewildering biographies of the spirit among his works." He was a trusted friend of Sand's and the "director of her literary conscience," as Chopin put it. Below these two portraits: the Bolshoi Theater in Moscow in a contemporary print. Czar Nicholas I invited Chopin to become court pianist, but the great Polish musician refused: he preferred remaining an émigré in Paris to giving pleasure with his music to those who, in 1831, had bloodily repressed the revolt of Warsaw.

"AT LAST MY EYES ARE OPEN"

When George Sand reappeared in Paris in the spring of 1847, something between her and Chopin that had appeared dead seemed to come to life again. She seemed in excellent spirits; after considering various ways to marry off Solange, she had the satisfaction of promising her restless daughter's hand to a worthy young man, a member of the landed gentry, who had fallen in love at first sight. But an unexpected character appeared on the scene: Jean Clésinger, 33 years old, an athletic if somewhat limited sculptor—Chopin immediately dubbed him the "cuirassier." This "handsome devil," while he was doing a portrait of Solange ("the grand duchess"), wooed and speedily seduced her. George and her daughter retired to the country, using Chopin's carriage for the journey. Clésinger did not strike Chopin as being a desirable suitor, and he did not hesitate to point this out to George; she, on the other hand, was enthusiastic. This romantic substitution of a Michelangelo for a landed proprietor was bound to appeal to her. Chopin, who had not been invited to the wedding at Nohant, and who was recov-

ering from a severe attack of asthma, sent his best wishes. It was soon evident that Chopin had correctly sized up the situation. George never forgave him for being right. Clésinger proved to be a violent man, good only at incurring debts. One evening a quarrel broke out. Clésinger, mallet in hand, lunged at Maurice, and struck George Sand. She threw the newlyweds out. Solange, who was expecting a baby, wanted to use Chopin's carriage, which her mother had kept at Nohant. George refused. Solange then appealed directly to Chopin, in Paris, who had no choice but to answer that it was at her disposal. George lost no time in seizing the pretext. She wrote to Chopin, urging him to break off with the Clésingers, but Chopin promised nothing. This was the last straw for Sand. She wrote to a friend: "The Clésingers and Chopin, who is supposed to be my most devoted friend: Splendid! . . . I know what Chopin's miserable little mind is capable of when it's a matter of credulity. But at last my eyes are open, and I shall never again allow my flesh and blood to be a pasture for ingratitude and perversity."

The year 1848, a great revolutionary time in Europe. On February 22, 1848, the people of Paris were again in arms on the streets. They went to Versailles. They demanded reforms. They sang the Marseillaise. Louis Philippe, King of the French, fled to Saint-Cloud (*print below*). He reached England incognito as Mr. Smith.

Center: The sack of the Tuileries, another episode of the Revolution of 1848 in Paris, shown in a contemporary print bearing the inscription: "Respect Christ, for he is your master." Above: Polish exiles leaving France to return home: Poland also was up in arms against Russia. Right: The Parisian mob invading the Tuileries.

"Friends came this morning to tell me that I ought to give a concert and not think of anything except to sit at the piano and play. The concert has been sold out for a week. The public is making plans for a second one I haven't even thought of as yet. The Court wanted forty tickets; all this expectation fills me with wonder. I must practice a little to quiet my conscience, because it seems to me I have never played so badly as now. Pleyel jokes about my stupidity and, to encourage me, promises to fill the room with flowers. It shall be as though I were at home and my eyes will see only familiar faces."

After the rupture with George Sand, in August, 1847, Chopin never stopped trying to re-create a life for himself. He went to the country with the Rothschilds, succumbed to what he described as a vile grippe, prepared for a concert. But his efforts were only half-hearted. He sent to the publisher, Breitkopf, three waltzes op. 64, three mazurkas op. 63, and the Sonata for Cello—the last compositions to appear while he was still alive. Around him the vacuum grew. Witwicki died. "And I? I shall end up by believing myself immortal," he had said with bitter irony when the 15-year-old Filchst died, the promising pupil for whom Liszt had prophesied a great future. As for George, she sent Chopin one last letter, which Delacroix refers to in his *Journal:* "A horrible letter in which cruel passions and long-repressed impatience come to the surface in a contrast that would be interesting if it were not this particular case." And she continued to make excuses for herself. "Since the Clésingers and Chopin will continue to blow the trumpets against us," she admonished Maurice, "you, too, must blow the truth in Mme Marliani's (ears). . . ." But this year, 1847, had been a bad one for her also. "Without Maurice," she was to confess later, "I should have taken my life."

And it was at the door of Mme Marliani, with whom they had enjoyed their best meals, that George Sand and Chopin met casually one last time in March, 1848. A little girl had been born to Solange; it was Chopin who announced the event to George Sand. "How are you?" "Well." That was all. They were never to see each other again.

THE HOUR OF
REVOLUTION

On February 12, 1848, "tout-Paris" came to the Salle Pleyel for what turned out to be Chopin's last concert in France. Chopin, who had not appeared on the concert stage for six years, played as he had never played before. It was as though he knew that he was celebrating not only his own apotheosis but also that of an entire society. The repeat performance, planned as a response to critical and public acclaim, never took place. On February 22, the Marseillaise was heard once more in the streets of Paris; once more the *garde nationale* went over to the side of the people. Revolution, the recurring motif in the life of Chopin, coincided this time with a crucial turning point in his life. Power passed into the hands of George Sand's friends of the new wave, among them Louis Blanc and Arago. Malefille, the former tutor at Nohant, became the director of Versailles. The King and "tout-Paris" quickly crossed the Channel.

With Louis Philippe gone, it was not only France that continued to be restless. As in 1831, the spirit of revolution was abroad throughout Europe. Some of its leaders were romantic poets, like Lamartine, the new head of the republican government. "We ask for news, as did the ancient Athenians, and the cannon booms its answer," said Zaleski. Poland, in 1846, had fired the opening salvo of the Revolution, and already many of her sons lay dead. The Polish struggle had struck chords of sympathy in France. The railroads gave free transportation up to the frontiers to volunteers on their way to Poznan, where Mieroslawski was putting together an army.

In Italy, Mickiewicz was forming another "Polish Legion." Like other exiles, Chopin lived through days of hope, despair and enthusiasm. For a fleeting moment he could again believe in his hope for the rebirth of Poland. "My compatriots are meeting in Poznan," he wrote to Fontana in April. "As a start, Czartoryski has gone. . . . Now everything reeks of war. The Italians have started. Milan has thrown out the Austrians. . . . The French will doubtless send reinforcements. The Muscovites will certainly run into trouble when they march against the Prussians. . . . This will not occur without terrible events, but at the end of all this there will be a splendid, a great Poland."

Above: The celebration at the proclamation of the Second Republic in Paris (February 24, 1848): Delacroix wrote about it: "The ox Apis, allegorical triumphal carts followed by 400 virgins: it took a revolution to produce so many marvels!" The head of the government, which was formed with the help of the socialist Ledru-Rollin, was Lamartine (on horseback, in print below), the author of Meditations. *Many of George Sand's friends came to power: Pierre Leroux, a philosopher and pamphleteer, who founded in 1839 with George Sand the* Revue Indépendante; *Arago and Louis Blanc, who inspired the labor movement and founded the national workshops; Malefille, former tutor at Nohant. Sand took a great deal of trouble to find posts for her friends. She also took an active part in politics, and had Maurice elected mayor of Nohant. Opposite page, above: Presentation to the National Assembly of a petition for Poland in revolt against Russia. Polish legions had been formed by Mickiewicz in Italy, by Chopin's friend Szulczewski in Turkey, by Mieroslawski in Poznan. Opposite page, below: A meeting of the Assembly of 1848.*

A WARM WELCOME IN LONDON

Chopin arrived in London on April 21, 1848. Jane Stirling, who had arranged his London expedition, settled him in a cozy apartment on Bentick Street that was even stocked with writing paper bearing his initials. This and other exquisite courtesies soon caused Chopin to move to 48 Dover Street; already there were too many rumors of an absurd marriage with this heiress who aspired to the role of George Sand II without being suited to the part. She was too attentive, too rich; she hadn't enough temperament.

Crossing the Channel was madness, in view of the smog and Chopin's health, but he wanted to break away from Paris after George Sand's defection, and he needed to give concerts to replenish his funds. The *Atheneum* commented that "we owe thanks to the new French Republic for this visit of Chopin's!" A real Parisian season was in full swing in London. There, Chopin found Kalkbrenner, Osborne, Thalberg and Mme Viardot Garcia, who sang some of his mazurkas at Covent Garden. He took the Swedish soprano, Jenny Lind, to dinner, discovering "that there existed a greater affinity between Slavs and Scandinavians than between Italians and Spaniards." He played at Stafford House, the stronghold of the Tory aristocracy, in the presence of Queen Victoria and the Prince Consort. He played with great success in more concerts. But he refused to appear with the Philharmonic, because the orchestra was "like their turtle soup, energetic, but nothing more. . . ." Furthermore, "in this country, where time is money," the orchestra rehearsed only once, and in public. Instead, he started giving lessons again, at the rate of one gold guinea a session. Again he had his own carriage waiting at the door. He also had a friend, James Broadwood, who was as solicitous as Fontana. "One evening, upon coming home, I found a new mattress and very soft pillows. . . . It was only after much insistence that I was able to persuade Daniel to tell me that they had been sent by Broadwood, who knew of my insomnia and had enjoined him to say nothing to me. . . ." Chopin led a very active social life. He met Dickens, Carlyle, Hogarth, Walter Scott. He allowed himself to be made much of by the ladies ("Lady Byron . . . how well I understand why her husband lives abroad!"). But, behind the brilliant façade: "If only I could leave off spitting blood for a while, if only I weren't a prey to an idiotic homesickness. . . . I vegetate, simply, and patiently await my end. . . ."

In April, 1848, when Chopin was already quite sick, he went to London. The drawing rooms of high society were thrown wide open for his "paid performances." He gave his first concert at 99 Eaton Place, the house of Mrs. Adelaide Sartoris, daughter of the famous actor, Kemble (500 tickets at a guinea apiece were sold); then he played at Lord Falmouth's house, 2 St. James' Square (left): "A great lover of music and a great lord; nonetheless one would be tempted to give him alms were one to meet him in the street; and at home also, he has a multitude of servants better dressed than he. . . ." He also performed at the Duchess of Sutherland's, where he was again acclaimed by the Atheneum. Only the critic of the Times, Davison, who thought Chopin a threat to his idol Mendelssohn, withheld his praise; he was later to make amends in a perceptive Essay on the Polish musician's art. Below: Regent Street, the heart of elegant London. It was here that Chopin's English publishers, Wessel and Stapleton, had their offices. Opposite page, from left: Walter Scott and Dickens, who admired Chopin.

London: The Italian Opera House in 1828 (below, in an etching by Shepard). Chopin appeared on November 16, 1848 at a concert and ball given at the Guildhall in the British capital for the benefit of Polish exiles (the two middle pictures on this page). It was the last time he was to appear in public. He had not wanted to disappoint Lord Stuart, president of the Association of the Friends of Poland. Bottom of page: View of Buckingham Palace. Opposite page: One aspect of English life in his day: Queen Victoria visits Somerset House.

In Calder House, 12 miles from Edinburgh, a huge room was set aside for Chopin; on the floor above, 300 years earlier, John Knox had prayed through the night. There was a Broadwood piano in his room. In the room next to his there was a Pleyel piano, sent by Jane Stirling. There was also, inevitably, a family ghost. But the musician, who spent a portion of the summer as Lord Thorpichen's guest of honor, was not to be disturbed. In the evenings Chopin played old Scottish airs for the master of the house, a member of the Stirling clan. And "he expressed his feelings to him in French." Calder House may well have been the most satisfying

lap of his British trip: galleries, acres of lawns, horses, almost like an Antonin Castle transplanted from Poland to Scotland. But it was useless to deceive oneself. From the haven where Miss Stirling would have liked to keep the beloved master, Chopin wrote to Fontana, "I haven't a single musical idea; I am like a donkey at a masked ball." And also: "We are two old cymbals on which time and circumstance have played their dismal tremolo . . . we can't give out new notes under clumsy hands, and we choke down in ourselves all that which, for the want of an expert lute player, no one can draw out of us. . . ."

A BUNCH OF VIOLETS

Opposite page, above: Stafford House, the residence of the Duke of Sutherland. Chopin played in a concert there before Queen Victoria, on May 15, 1848. It was said that the Queen, incognito, took lessons from him. Opposite, below: Balmoral, in Scotland, the summer residence of England's rulers during the past century. Directly below: Drawing room of an English country house; the water color is by Lami. Chopin came into contact with Scottish county society when he was staying at Stirling Castle (bottom of the page). "There are only male and female cousins of great families here," he wrote to Grzymala, "conversation is limited to genealogy: so and so is related to thus and such, and this one to that one, and so on. . . ."

Chopin was dying of depression in Scotland, despite his hosts' kindness. He was never again to hear from his irreplaceable "lute player"—George Sand—after his wretched meeting with her at the door of Mme Marliani's house. And Jane Stirling could give him no strength; on the contrary, she sought it from him. After barely three weeks, Chopin left Calder House. The tour he took seemed calculated to finish him off. He played in Manchester and in Glasgow. With a flash of his old spirit, he tried to keep Osborne from coming to hear him in the concert hall in Edinburgh: "I should like to leave you with the impression I made on you in Paris. . . ." Finally, in the autumn, he returned to London, where he seldom left his bed. Mrs. Erskine, Jane Stirling's sister, used to read him the Psalms, observing that "the next world is certainly better than this one." "One more day here," Chopin wrote to Grzymala, "and I shall go mad. My Scottish ladies exasperate me so." Queen Victoria's personal physician, Sir James Clark, was by now also attending him. Finally Chopin made up his mind: He wrote to Grzymala, "Order a bunch of violets for Friday, so that I may still find a little poetry when I come back. . . ."

69

Below: Photograph of Chopin taken a few months before his death; the ravages of sickness are evident. The Manchester Guardian *wrote, after the concert he gave on August 30, 1848: "He is very spare in frame, and there is an almost painful air of feebleness in his appearance and gait." Right: Alessio Jelowicki, a fellow student of Chopin's.*

"HE WAS AS HANDSOME AS EVER"

"I had gone to see him, and I was about to leave, because I was told that he was sleeping. When it was known who I was," reports Norwid, the poet, "Chopin asked me to come up again. . . . In the shadow of the bed hangings he was as handsome as ever, there was something sculptural about him. . . . As he greeted me, he said: 'I shall move,' and he began to cough. I replied: 'You move like this every year, and always, thank Heaven, we find you alive.' And, disregarding the coughing, he continued: 'No, I tell you, I'll move from here to go to the Place Vendôme. . . .'"

Chopin kept his word. He lived at 12 Place Vendôme from October 1 to 17, 1849. The months before this move fled by, in preparation for the end. After a painful winter, the month of May saw a deceptive improvement in his health. He had reached the highest peak of his artistry, composing luminous music—the Barcarolle, the Berceuse—which conjured up no ghosts, no hint of death. He struggled on to the very end with his customary insouciance. In June, he moved to Chaillot, where he could look upon green grass and trees. It was as close a substitute for past summers at Nohant as he could afford, for his funds were very low. The house was spacious and airy: "Besides the gardens I can see before me all of Paris, the Tuileries, Notre Dame, St. Étienne, the Invalides. . . ." Paris was still his favorite place of exile. The good weather saw him up and around again, elegant as always. He went to the Bois with Norwid, and was once more seen in Polish circles. He questioned Mickiewicz, who was back from Italy, and wrangled with Slowacki, the author of *Lilla Weneda* ("that peacock, that fool"), who was to die the same year. He went to the theater to shudder conscientiously at the premiere of Meyerbeer's *Prophet*. And, while cholera raged (Kalkbrenner was a victim), he had a friend read to him from Voltaire's *Dictionnaire Philosophique*. Many friends came to call: Léo, Pleyel, Mme Kalergi, his last pupil, the enchantress Delphine. And, in August, he was overjoyed by the arrival of his sister, Louise, who came rushing from Warsaw to be by his side.

Left: The drawing room of 12 Place Vendôme; Chopin died there, on October 17, 1849, of tuberculosis of the larynx and the lungs. Liszt wrote of Chopin's preludes: "Admirable in their diversity, and in the work and knowledge they reveal, they can only be appreciated after painstaking examination. Everything seems to be a first flush, an impulse, a sudden rush. They have the freedom and breath which characterize works of genius." Above: The Gare St. Lazare in 1848.

In contrast to the squalid funeral of Chopin's idol Mozart, the Polish musician's was almost a social event: About 3,000 people were present, including musical and literary society, ladies of fashion, and the English and French press. "Nature had a festive air," reporters wrote. Mozart's Requiem was sung, according to Chopin's wish, by Mme Viardot Garcia and Lablache in the Church of the Madeleine. It was a dazzling performance: "How the master would have appreciated it," the admiring chronicler of the Illustration Française wrote. Chopin was buried in the Père Lachaise cemetery. A handful of Polish soil accompanied him into the French earth. Jane Stirling saw to everything. The woman who was aptly described as "Chopin's widow" came to Père Lachaise the following year in complete privacy. She was one of the few who appreciated the funeral monument made by Clésinger. Below: Chopin's death, by Kniatowski.

"SUBLIME SONG OF ALL SUFFERING"

Below, left: Barria's version of Chopin's death. Delphine Potocka's beauty and her solicitousness were a comfort to him until the very end. Elegantly dressed in white, the "enchantress" sang a hymn by Stradello and a Psalm of Benedetto Marcello's. Right: Chopin's hand—a cast, by Clésinger.

The years between 1840 and 1845 marked the high point of Chopin's artistic productivity. He was then living with George Sand, who, with her children, had given him the illusion of having a home. Among the first works of this period were: the Sonata in B flat minor Op. 35; the Impromptu in F sharp major Op. 36; the Scherzo Op. 39; the Polonaises in A flat, in C minor, in F sharp minor; the Fantaisie Op. 49; the Nocturne in G minor. The Sonata Op. 35 was a departure from the sonata form established by Beethoven, which had once been considered the ultimate development of the form. It was disconcerting for Chopin's contemporaries; Schumann called it "the smile of the sphinx." "The idea of calling it a sonata is a caprice, if not a jest, for he has simply bound together four of his most reckless children." Especially "reckless" were the last two movements: the *marche funèbre*, and the tumultuous finale, a relentless demented presto, one of the most personal, bizarre poems ever dedicated by a romantic to death. It contains everything: anguish, demonism, sarcasm and even a touch of the baroque; "winds of night sweeping over churchyard graves" was Anton Rubinstein's description. "Chopin," said Legouvé, "never refused to play it, but hardly was the last bar finished, than he used to reach for his hat and leave. . . ." "Out of balance" in the opinion of some, the sonata is undeniably one of the most suggestive pieces of music ever written. Pianists have not always known how to interpret it. Some, with an extraordinary talent for identifying themselves with the music, succeed in literally galvanizing the audience with this sonata. Others dominate it with an interpretation that is almost starched, unyielding, peremptory and eloquent. The Sonata in B minor Op. 58, composed in 1845, is in complete contrast to this "poem of death," which was described by Ganche as the "sublime song of all suffering, the desperate hymn of a dying world." The later Sonata Op. 58 is rather the work of a romantic who adores the classics, who, as he gradually approaches death, refuses to dramatize it, and rises disdainfully above it; it is lighter, less agonized. Developed in classical style, it is alien to the kind of romantic suffering and macabre fantasies that could drive someone like Schumann to despair.

Chopin, standing in the center, is surrounded by well-known pianists of his day. From the left, standing: Rosenhain, Döhler, Chopin, Dreyschock, Thalberg; seated: Wolff, Henselt, Liszt. It was Paganini who taught the pianists a new technique for virtuosity on the piano, an instrument ideally suited to romanticism. Alfred Einstein wrote: "Transposing his virtuoso techniques to their instrument, the pianists—from Chopin to Liszt, to Schumann, to Brahms— tried to eliminate the normal differences between piano and violin techniques."

J. Rosenhain   F. Döhler   F. Chopin   A. Dreyschock   S. Thalberg

E. Wolff   A. Henselt   F. Liszt

Much has been written on Chopin, and his figure has been variously illuminated from time to time. Actually, Chopin was an introverted genius whose music was highly individual and personal. He cared nothing for setting patterns or devising formulas for the production of universal works of art of the type in which Wagner excelled. Chopin's contribution to the evolution of music is nonetheless great. His work in harmony is the basis for much modern orchestration. He was an intensely lyrical composer who gave free rein to self-expression. He was thought by some to be out of his element in compositions of large scope, such as the concerto. Fortunately, he knew his limitations, and confined the greater part of his work to the smaller forms: nocturnes, études, preludes, dances (polonaises, mazurkas, waltzes). It was in these that he found the happiest expression of his genius, and it is no doubt one of the reasons for the popularity of his music for drawing-room playing. Despite the often strongly pronounced Polish national characteristics of his music, it is also expressive of his own emotions and sufferings, and thereby achieves the universality characteristic of any true masterpiece. Debussy said that Chopin evades "the game of classifications." He does, indeed, rise above historic or aesthetic categories, for his music has the formal perfection, clarity and balance of classicism, while at the same time it reveals the inspired vision and inner mystery of the human heart.

1810—February 22: Born at Zelazowa Wola, near Warsaw: second child of Nicolas Chopin, native of Marainville in Lorraine, teacher of French, and of Justine Krzyzanowska, a Polish lady. He had three sisters: Ludwika (Louise), Isabelle, Emily.

1811—Franz Liszt is born in Doborjàn, Hungary.

1815—After three previous partitions in 1772, 1793 and 1795, Poland is once more dismembered by the Russians, the Prussians and the Austrians.

1818—February 24: Chopin, aged eight, gives his first concert in Warsaw.

1823—Studies harmony and counterpoint with Josef Elsner, who is also to be his teacher at the Warsaw Conservatory until 1829.

1826—August: Short stay in Reinertz, a small spa in Silesia, where his sister Emily is taking a cure. She dies of consumption the following year.

1829—August: Chopin gives two concerts in Vienna. Back in Warsaw, he starts work again on his Concerto in E minor and on some of his études.

1830—March 17, March 22, October 11: He gives three concerts before leaving Poland. He is restless because of his love for Costantia Gladkowska, a young singer he has met at the Conservatory, and for whom he composes the Larghetto of Concerto Op. 21 and the Waltz Op. 70. November 2, All Saints Day: Frédéric Chopin leaves Poland forever. Homesickness for his native land (he takes with him a fistful of Polish soil in a silver box) is to stay with him for the whole of his life. In November,

Warsaw rises up against the autocracy of Czar Nicholas I of Russia.

1831—September 8: The Russians, under the command of General Paskievic, reoccupy Warsaw. Mid-September: Chopin settles in Paris, after spending almost nine months in Vienna and two months in various German cities.

1832—February and March: Two concerts at the Salle Pleyel reveal Chopin's greatness to the elite of Paris. Finishes the Etudes Op. 10. From this year until 1836, he composes, among other pieces, Scherzo Op. 20, Ballade Op. 23, Rondo Op. 16, Mazurkas Op. 24, Nocturnes Op. 27.

1835—Sees his parents again at Karlsbad, where they have gone to take the cure. Then, in Dresden, he sees Maria Wodzinska, his first piano pupil in Warsaw, for whom he has always had a deep affection. He composes the Valse d' Adieu for her. He plays with Hiller and Liszt in various concerts.

1836—Summer: Chopin asks for the hand of Maria Wodzinska, but the following autumn he receives through her mother a veiled refusal from the girl. The reason for this is the apprehension of Maria's parents about Chopin's precarious health. November: First meeting with George Sand, in the Liszt household.

1837—Brief stay in London with Camille Pleyel.

1838—November: Chopin and Sand in the Balearic Islands. They live first in Palma di Majorca in the villa Son Vent, then at the Chartreuse di Valdemosa. Here he composes the 24 preludes, Scherzo Op. 39, Im-

promptu Op. 36, Polonaise Op. 40, Mazurkas Op. 41.

1839—June: Because of the inclement weather, Chopin returns to France and spends the summer in Nohant at Sand's home. He is to return here for successive summers, spending the winters in Paris. Composes Sonata B flat minor Op. 35—which contains the famous *Marche Funèbre*—a nocturne and four mazurkas.

1841—April 26: Another concert at the Salle Pleyel in Paris, this time as soloist. Liszt writes an enthusiastic review. Chopin's health, meantime, continues to deteriorate, but he nonetheless goes through a period of intense inspiration and composes his Polonaise in A major, Ballade in A flat major, three mazurkas and two nocturnes. These are some of his most important works.

1844—A sad year: The death of his father, the advance of his disease, quarrels with George Sand.

1847—August: Break with George Sand.

1848—February 12: Chopin's last concert in Paris. April: At the insistence of one of his admirers, the Scottish lady Jane Stirling, he crosses the Channel and gives, in London and in other cities in England and Scotland, his last concerts.

1849—October 17: Death of Frédéric Chopin in Paris. Before the end he asks his older sister Louise (who has been present at his death bed) to take his heart back to Poland. The mortal remains of the great musician are buried, at his request, in the Père Lachaise cemetery in Paris, not far from the graves of Bellini and Cherubini.

The works reproduced in this volume can be found in the following collections: Chantilly, Musée Condé: p. 27. Dresden, State Museum: p. 35. Dunrobin Castle (Scotland), Countess of Sutherland Collection: p. 67. London: British Museum: pp. 31, 64, 65, 66, 68, 69; Guildhall: p. 66; Victoria and Albert Museum: pp. 30, 69. Milan, Bertarelli Collection: p. 24. Nohant, Musée La Chatre: pp. 36, 41, 45, 46, 53, 54, 55, 56; Paris: Institut de France: pp. 48, 51, 53, 54, 56; Polish Library: pp. 22, 30, 32, 33, 42, 46; Musée Carnavalet: pp. 24, 25, 26, 29, 45, 46-47, 48, 50-51, 52, 56-57, 58-59, 59, 60, 62, 63, 71, 73; Bibliothèque Nationale: pp. 12, 27, 28, 30, 32, 35, 37, 42-43, 50, 61, 62, 63, 70. Bibliothèque de l'Opéra: pp. 19, 25, 28, 42, 56; Louvre: pp. 22, 37, 53; Louvre Cabinet des desseins: p. 59. Warsaw: National Museum: pp. 4-5, 9, 10-11, 12-13, 15, 17; Archives of the Chopin Society: pp. 4, 6, 8, 10, 11, 12, 14, 15, 16, 17, 18, 19, 20, 31, 33, 34, 50, 72-73. Versailles, Musée: pp. 23, 44, 46, 47. Vienna, City Museum: pp. 20, 21. Picture research: Georgina Bruckner. Photographic reference: Arborio Mella: pp. 38, 40. Carabelli: end papers. Del Grande: frontispiece, pp. 6, 6-7, 8, 14, 16, 18, 19, 33, 72-73. Electra Cliché: pp. 4-5, 6, 10-11, 12-13, 15, 17. Freeman: pp. 30, 31, 56, 64, 65, 66, 68, 69. Giraudon: pp. 22, 25, 26, 35, 37, 44. Meyer: pp. 20, 21. Scarnati: pp. 12, 19, 22, 23, 24, 25, 27, 28, 29, 30, 31, 32, 33, 35, 36, 37, 40, 41, 42, 42-43, 45, 46, 47, 48, 49, 50-51, 51, 52, 53, 54, 55, 56, 57, 58-59, 59, 60, 61, 62, 63, 70, 71, 73; and the Mondadori Photographic Archives.